easy meals

low fat

p

This is a Parragon Publishing Book
This edition published in 2004

Parragon Publishing
Queen Street House
4 Queen Street
Bath BA1 1HE, UK

ISBN: 1-40541-508-8

Printed in China

Produced by The Bridgewater Book Company Ltd, Lewes, East Sussex

Creative Director Terry Jeavons
Art Director Sarah Howerd
Page Make-up Sara Kidd
Editorial Director Fiona Biggs
Senior Editor Mark Truman
Editorial Assistant Tom Kitch

NOTES FOR THE READER

- This book uses both metric and US measurements. Follow the same units of measurement throughout; do not mix metric and US measurements.
- All spoon measurements are level: teaspoons are assumed to be 5 ml, and table-spoons are assumed to be 15 ml.
- Cup measurements in this book are for American cups.
- Unless otherwise stated, milk is assumed to be whole milk, eggs and individual vegetables such as potatoes are medium-sized, and pepper is freshly ground black pepper.
- Recipes using raw or very lightly cooked eggs should be avoided by infants, the elderly, pregnant women, convalescents, and anyone suffering from an illness.
- Optional ingredients, variations, and serving suggestions have not been included in the calculations.
- The times given are an approximate guide only. Preparation times differ according to the techniques used by different people and the cooking times vary as a result of the type of oven used.

Contents

Introduction

Changing your diet to lower its fat content may sound like a
a challenge, but it will not be difficult if you adopt a positive
attitude. You simply need to adjust your cooking methods and
make use of some of the inspiring recipe ideas in this book. All
the dishes are easy to prepare and cook, so you will not need to
resort to unhealthy fast food even when time is short, as on mid-
week evenings. The recipes have been gathered from cultures
ranging from Thai, Chinese and Indian to Mediterranean and
Mexican, so you can try out some exciting new ideas while you
cut down on your cholesterol intake. This lifestyle change will
not leave you feeling disadvantaged.

The recipes rely heavily on ingredients which are naturally low in
fat, such as fish, chicken, lean meat, fresh vegetables, beans,
and foods such as pasta which are high in energy-giving
carbohydrates. They also use lowfat milk, yogurt, cheese, and
margarine, all readily available. Butter does not appear, but

guide to recipe key	
easy	Recipes are graded as follows: 1 pea = easy; 2 peas = very easy; 3 peas = extremely easy.
serves 4	Recipes generally serve four people. Halve the ingredients to serve two, taking care not to mix US and metric measurements.
15 minutes	Preparation time. Where recipes include marinating, these times are separately noted: eg, 15 minutes, plus 30 minutes to marinate.
15 minutes	Cooking time. Cooking times do not include the cooking of rice or noodles served with the main dishes.

olive oil – an important ingredient in the healthy Mediterranean food – is included in small amounts. The recipes also make good use of flavorings and seasonings. A dish can be transformed with fresh, fragrant herbs, hot chiles, pungent garlic, zesty ginger root, and warming spices.

Dinner parties and weekend brunches and lunches are times when you may feel inclined to indulge in fatty foods. Instead, devote time to planning a special menu. Vietnamese Rice Paper Wraps, followed by Beef & Peppers with Lemon Grass and a Lychee & Ginger Sorbet is one suggestion for turning a low-fat meal into a gastronomic occasion.

Chicken & Mango Stir-Fry, page 30

Soups & Appetizers

It is very easy to create a low-fat appetizer. Simple soups are an obvious first choice. Made simply from vegetables, beans, lean meat, or fish cooked in stock, they may still be impressive if exotically flavored and garnished. Alternatively, use fruit or raw vegetable juice. Cold Tomato, Carrot & Orange Soup is the healthiest appetizer, entirely fat-free, and made from raw ingredients, so all the goodness is retained. For a more exotic, elegant appetizer, serve Lemon Grass Chicken Skewers. With skewers made from lemon grass stems and garnished with cilantro and lime, they make a delicious talking point.

Sweet & Sour Cabbage Soup

INGREDIENTS

½ cup golden raisins
½ cup orange juice
1 tbsp olive oil
1 large onion, chopped
3 cups shredded
    cabbage
2 apples, peeled and
    diced
½ cup apple juice
14 oz/400 g canned
    peeled tomatoes in
    juice
1 cup tomato or
    vegetable juice
3½ oz/100 g pineapple
    flesh, chopped finely
5 cups water
2 tsp wine vinegar
salt and pepper
fresh mint leaves,
    to garnish

❶ Put the golden raisins in a bowl, then pour the orange juice over them and let stand for 15 minutes.

❷ Heat the oil in a large pan over a medium heat. Add the onion, cover, and cook for 3–4 minutes, stirring frequently, until the onion starts to soften. Add the cabbage and cook for another 2 minutes; do not let it brown.

❸ Add the apples and apple juice, then cover and cook gently for 5 minutes. Stir in the tomatoes, tomato juice, pineapple, and water. Season with salt and pepper, and add the vinegar.

❹ Add the golden raisins and the orange juice. Bring to a boil, then reduce the heat and simmer, partially covered, for about 1 hour, or until the fruit and vegetables are tender.

❺ Let the soup cool slightly, then transfer to a blender or a food processor and purée until smooth; work in batches if necessary. (If using a food processor, strain off the liquid and reserve. Purée the soup solids with enough liquid to moisten them, then combine with the remaining liquid.)

❻ Return the soup to the pan and simmer gently for about 10 minutes to reheat. Ladle into warm bowls. Garnish with mint leaves and serve immediately.

 easy

 serves 4

 20 minutes, plus
15 minutes to
soak raisins

1½ hours

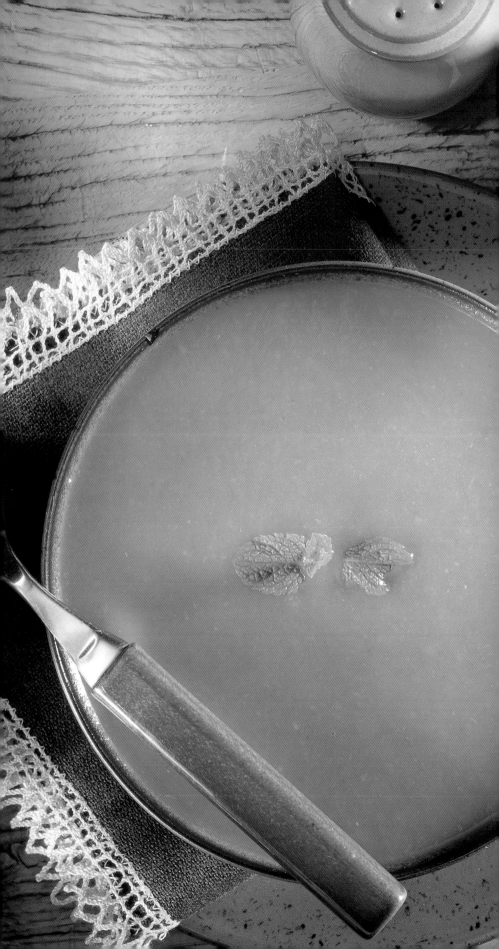

Fennel & Tomato Soup with Shrimp

2 tsp olive oil
1 large onion, halved and sliced
2 large fennel bulbs, halved and sliced
1 small potato, diced
3¾ cups water
1¾ cups tomato juice
1 bay leaf
4½ oz/125 g cooked shelled small shrimp
2 tomatoes, skinned, deseeded, and chopped
½ tsp snipped fresh dill
salt and pepper
dill sprigs or fennel fronds, to garnish

1 Heat the olive oil in a large pan over a medium heat. Add the onion and fennel, and cook for 3–4 minutes, stirring occasionally, until the onion is just softened.

2 Add the potato, water, tomato juice, and bay leaf, and a large pinch of salt. Reduce the heat, cover, and simmer for about 25 minutes, stirring once or twice, until the vegetables are soft.

3 Let the mixture cool slightly, then transfer to a blender or a food processor and purée until the soup is smooth, working in batches if necessary. (If using a food processor, strain off the cooking liquid and reserve. Purée the soup solids with enough cooking liquid to moisten them, then combine with the remaining liquid.)

4 Return the soup to the pan and add the shrimp. Simmer gently for about 10 minutes to reheat the soup and let it absorb the shrimp flavor.

5 Stir in the tomatoes and dill. Taste and add salt and pepper, if needed. If the soup seems too thick, thin it with a little more tomato juice. Ladle the soup into warm bowls, then garnish with dill or fennel fronds, and serve.

easy

serves 4

20 minutes

50 minutes

Chinese Pork Balls & Greens in Broth

INGREDIENTS

8 cups chicken bouillon
3 oz/85 g shiitake
  mushrooms, sliced
  thinly
6 oz/175 g bok choy or
  other Asian greens,
  sliced into thin
  ribbons
6 scallions, sliced finely
salt and pepper

PORK BALLS
225 g/8 oz lean ground
  pork
25 g/1 oz fresh spinach
  leaves, chopped finely
2 scallions, chopped
  finely
1 garlic clove, chopped
  very finely
pinch of 5-spice powder
1 tsp soy sauce

❶ To make the pork balls, put the pork, spinach, scallions, and garlic in a bowl. Add the 5-spice powder and soy sauce, and mix until combined.

❷ Shape the pork mixture into 24 balls. Place them in one layer in a steamer that will fit over the top of a cooking pan.

❸ Bring the bouillon just to a boil in a pan that will accommodate the steamer. Regulate the heat so the liquid bubbles gently. Add the mushrooms to the bouillon, and place the steamer, covered, on top of the pan. Steam for 10 minutes. Remove the steamer and set aside on a plate.

❹ Add the bok choy and scallions to the pan and cook them gently in the bouillon for 3–4 minutes, or until the leaves are wilted. Taste the soup and adjust the seasoning, if necessary.

❺ Divide the pork balls evenly among 6 warm bowls and ladle the soup over them. Serve at once.

 very easy

 makes 24

 20 minutes

15 minutes

Greek Bean Soup with Lemon & Mint

INGREDIENTS

1 tbsp olive oil
1 large onion, chopped
   finely
1 large carrot, diced
   finely
2 celery stalks, chopped
   finely
4 tomatoes, skinned,
   deseeded, and
   chopped, or 9 oz/
   250 g drained canned
   tomatoes
2 garlic cloves, chopped
   finely
1 lb 12 oz/800 g canned
   cannellini or Great
   Northern beans,
   drained and rinsed well
5 cups water
1 zucchini, diced finely
grated zest of ½ lemon
1 tbsp chopped fresh
   mint, or ¼ tsp dried
   mint
1 tsp chopped fresh
   thyme, or ⅛ tsp dried
   thyme
1 bay leaf
14 oz/400 g canned
   artichoke hearts
salt and pepper

❶ Heat 1 teaspoon of the olive oil in a large pan over a medium heat. Add the onion and cook for 3–4 minutes, stirring occasionally, until the onion softens. Add the carrot, celery, tomatoes, and garlic and continue cooking for another 5 minutes, stirring frequently.

❷ Add the beans and water. Bring to a boil, then reduce the heat, cover, and cook gently for about 10 minutes.

❸ Add the zucchini, lemon zest, mint, thyme, and bay leaf, and season with salt and pepper. Cover, and simmer for about 40 minutes, or until all the vegetables are tender. Let cool slightly. Transfer 2 cups to a blender or a food processor, purée until smooth, then recombine.

❹ Meanwhile, heat the remaining oil in a skillet over a medium heat, adding more if necessary to coat the bottom of the skillet. Cook the artichokes, cut side down in the skillet, until lightly browned. Turn them over and cook long enough to heat the artichokes through.

❺ Ladle the soup into warm bowls and top each portion with an artichoke heart.

easy

serves 4

20 minutes

1 hour

Cold Tomato, Carrot, & Orange Soup

INGREDIENTS

3 large seedless oranges
4 ripe tomatoes
2 celery stalks, strings
*   removed, chopped*
3 carrots, grated
1½ cups tomato juice
salt
Tabasco sauce (optional)
1 tbsp chopped fresh
*   mint*
fresh mint sprigs, to
*   garnish*

❶ Working over a bowl to catch the juices, peel the oranges. Cut down between the membranes and drop the orange segments into the bowl.

❷ Put the tomatoes in a small bowl and pour boiling water over to cover them. Let stand for 10 seconds, then drain. Peel off the skin and cut the tomatoes in half crosswise. Scoop out the seeds into a strainer set over a bowl. Reserve the tomato juices.

❸ Put the tomatoes, celery, and carrots in a blender (or a food processor). Add the orange segments and their juice, plus the juice saved from the tomatoes. Purée until smooth.

❹ Scrape into a bowl and stir in the tomato juice. Cover and chill until cold.

 very easy

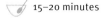 serves 24

 15–20 minutes

🕐 16 minutes

❺ Taste the soup and add salt, and a few drops of Tabasco sauce if necessary to heighten the flavor. Stir in the chopped mint, then ladle the soup into cold bowls, and garnish with fresh mint sprigs.

COOK'S TIP

This soup really needs to be made in a blender for the best texture. A food processor can be used, but the soup will not be completely smooth.

Griddled Smoked Salmon

INGREDIENTS

12 oz/350 g sliced
smoked salmon
1 tsp Dijon mustard
1 garlic clove, crushed
2 tsp chopped fresh dill
2 tsp sherry vinegar
4 tbsp olive oil
4 oz/115 g mixed salad
leaves
salt and pepper

❶ Take the slices of smoked salmon and fold them, making two folds accordion-style, so that they form little parcels.

❷ Whisk the mustard, garlic, dill, vinegar, and seasoning together. Gradually whisk in the olive oil to form a light emulsion.

❸ Heat a ridged griddle until it smokes. Cook the salmon bundles on one side only for 2–3 minutes, or until they are heated through and marked from the pan.

❹ Meanwhile, dress the salad leaves with some of the vinaigrette and divide them between 4 serving plates. Top with the cooked smoked salmon, cooked side up. Drizzle with the remaining dressing.

 extremely easy

 serves 4

 5 minutes

 2–3 minutes

Vietnamese Rice Paper Wraps

INGREDIENTS

8 oz/225 g cooked
   shelled shrimp
8 oz/225 g salmon fillet,
   seared for 1 minute
   each side and cut into
   ¼ inch/5 mm slices
225 g/8 oz tuna steak,
   seared for 1 minute
   each side and cut into
   ¼ inch/5 mm slices
2 ripe avocados, peeled,
   sliced, and sprinkled
   with lime juice
6–8 asparagus tips,
   blanched
1 small red onion, sliced
   thinly
16 scallions, sliced
12 black Niçoise olives,
   sliced
14 cherry tomatoes,
   halved
large bunch of cilantro,
   leaves stripped from
   the stems
20–30 rice paper
   wrappers, preferably
   7 inch/18 cm circles
lime wedges

❶ To make the dipping sauces, put the ingredients for each into separate bowls and stir together to blend.

❷ Arrange the shrimp, fish, vegetables, and cilantro leaves on a large serving plate in groups, ready to use as different fillings for the wrappers. Cover loosely with plastic wrap and chill until ready to serve.

❸ Dip each wrapper very briefly into a bowl of warm water to soften it. Lay the wrappers on clean dish towels to absorb any excess water, then pile them onto a serving plate and cover with a damp dish towel.

❹ To serve, let the guests fill their own wrappers. Offer lime wedges for squeezing over the fillings, and pass the dipping sauces around separately.

SPICED VINEGAR DIPPING SAUCE:
scant ⅓ cup rice vinegar
2 tbsp Thai fish sauce
2 tbsp superfine sugar
1 garlic clove, chopped finely
2 red chiles, deseeded and sliced
   thinly
2 tbsp chopped fresh cilantro

SOY DIPPING SAUCE:
½ cup Thai fish sauce
4–6 tbsp lime juice
2 tbsp Japanese soy sauce
2–3 tbsp light brown sugar
1 inch/2.5 cm piece fresh ginger root,
   chopped finely
2–4 garlic cloves, crushed

extremely easy

serves 4

25–30 minutes

5 minutes

Lemon Grass Chicken Skewers

INGREDIENTS

2 long or 4 short lemon grass stems
2 large boneless, skinless chicken breasts (halves), about 14 oz/400 g in total
1 small egg white
1 carrot, grated finely
1 small red chile, deseeded and chopped
2 tbsp fresh garlic chives, chopped
2 tbsp fresh cilantro, chopped
1 tbsp sunflower oil
salt and pepper
cilantro and lime slices, to garnish

❶ If the lemon grass stems are long, cut them in half across the middle to make 4 short lengths. Cut each stalk in half lengthwise, so you have 8 sticks.

❷ Chop the chicken pieces coarsely and place them in a food processor with the egg white. Process to a smooth paste, then add the carrot, chile, chives, cilantro, and salt and pepper. Process for a few seconds to mix well.

❸ Chill the mixture in the refrigerator for about 15 minutes. Divide the mixture into 8 equal portions, and use your hands to shape the mixture around the skewers made from lemon grass stems.

❹ Brush the skewers with oil, and broil them under a preheated medium-hot broiler for 4–6 minutes, turning them occasionally, until they are golden brown and cooked thoroughly. Alternatively, grill them over medium-hot coals.

❺ Serve the chicken skewers hot, and garnished with cilantro and slices of lime.

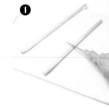

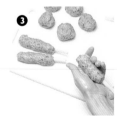

very easy

makes 8

20 minutes, plus 15 minutes to chill

4–6 minutes

Main
Meals

Stir-frying is an excellent way of cooking meat, fish and vegetables in the minimum of fat. It is also a fast cooking method, so you may take only minutes to make an attractive dish that tastes sensational. There are several great ideas for stir-fries in this part of the book. Try the Sauté of Chicken, Corn, & Snow peas for a mix of flavors combined with interesting texture. Steaming is the ideal cooking method for a healthy, low-fat diet. Steamed Yellow Fish Fillets, spicy and colorful, are an unusual and lower fat alternative to battered, fried fish.

Beef & Bell Peppers with Lemon Grass

1 lb 2 oz/500 g lean beef
    tenderloin
2 tbsp vegetable oil
1 garlic clove, chopped
    finely
1 lemon grass stem,
    shredded finely
1 inch/2.5 cm piece fresh
    ginger root, chopped
    finely
1 red bell pepper,
    deseeded and sliced
    thickly
1 green bell pepper,
    deseeded and sliced
    thickly
1 onion, sliced thickly
2 tbsp lime juice
boiled noodles or rice,
    to serve

❶ Cut the beef into long, thin strips, cutting across the grain.

❷ Heat the oil in a large skillet or wok over a high heat. Add the garlic and stir-fry for 1 minute.

❸ Add the beef and stir-fry for another 2–3 minutes, or until lightly colored. Stir in the lemon grass and ginger, and remove the wok from the heat.

❹ Remove the beef from the skillet or wok, and keep to one side. Add the bell peppers and onion to the skillet or wok, and stir-fry over a high heat for 2–3 minutes, or until the onions just turn golden brown and are slightly softened.

❺ Return the beef to the skillet, stir in the lime juice, and season to taste with salt and pepper. Serve with noodles or rice.

 extremely easy

 serves 4

 15 minutes

 15 minutes

Roasted Red Pork

INGREDIENTS

1 lb 5 oz/600 g pork
   fillets
bok choy, shredded to
   serve
red chile flower, to
   garnish

MARINADE
2 garlic cloves, crushed
1 tbsp fresh ginger root,
   grated
1 tbsp light soy sauce
1 tbsp Thai fish sauce
1 tbsp rice wine
1 tbsp hoi-sin sauce
1 tbsp sesame oil
1 tbsp palm sugar or
   brown sugar
½ tsp 5-spice powder
a few drops red food
   coloring (optional)

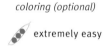 extremely easy

serves 4

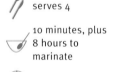 10 minutes, plus
8 hours to
marinate

1 hour

❶ Mix all the ingredients for the marinade together and spread over the pork, turning to coat evenly. Place in a large dish, then cover, and leave in the refrigerator to marinate overnight.

❷ Place a rack in a roasting pan, then half-fill the pan with boiling water. Lift the pork from the marinade and place it on the rack. Reserve the marinade for later use.

❸ Roast in a preheated oven at 425°F/220°C for about 20 minutes. Baste with the marinade, then lower the heat to 350°F/180°C and continue roasting for another 35–40 minutes, basting occasionally with the marinade, until the pork is a rich reddish brown and thoroughly cooked.

❹ Cut the pork into slices and serve it on a bed of shredded bok choy, garnished with a red chile flower.

 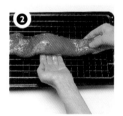 

COOK'S TIP
The pork may also be broiled. Cut the meat into slices or strips and coat in the marinade, then arrange on a foil-lined broiler pan and broil under a high heat, turning occasionally and basting with marinade.

Chicken & Mango Stir-Fry

6 boneless, skinless
  chicken thighs
1 inch/2.5 cm piece fresh
  ginger root, grated
1 garlic clove, crushed
1 small red chile,
  deseeded
1 large red bell pepper
4 scallions
7 oz/200 g snow peas
3½ oz/100 g baby corn
  cobs
1 large, firm, ripe mango
2 tbsp sunflower oil
1 tbsp light soy sauce
3 tbsp rice wine or sherry
1 tsp sesame oil
salt and pepper
sliced chives, to garnish

❶ Cut the chicken into long, thin strips and place them in a bowl. Mix together the ginger, garlic, and chile, then stir the mixture into the chicken strips to coat them evenly.

❷ Slice the bell pepper thinly, cutting diagonally. Trim the scallions and slice them diagonally. Cut the snow peas and corn in half diagonally. Peel the mango and remove the pit, and slice it thinly.

❸ Heat the oil in a large skillet or wok over a high heat. Add the chicken and stir-fry for 4–5 minutes, or until it just turns golden brown. Add the bell peppers and stir-fry over a medium heat for 4–5 minutes to soften them.

❹ Add the scallions, snow peas, and corn, and stir-fry for another minute.

❺ Mix the soy sauce, rice wine or sherry, and sesame oil and stir the mixture into the wok. Add the mango and stir gently for 1 minute to heat thoroughly.

❻ Adjust the seasoning with salt and pepper to taste, garnish with the sliced chives, and serve immediately.

 easy

serves 4

15 minutes

15 minutes

Rice Noodles with Chicken & Bok Choy

INGREDIENTS

7 oz/200 g rice stick
    noodles
1 tbsp sunflower oil
1 garlic clove, chopped
    finely
¼ inch/2 cm piece fresh
    ginger root, chopped
    finely
4 scallions, chopped
1 red bird-eye chile,
    deseeded and sliced
10½ oz/300 g boneless,
    skinless chicken,
    chopped finely
2 chicken livers, chopped
    finely
1 celery stalk, sliced thinly
1 carrot, cut into short,
    thin sticks
10½ oz/300 g shredded
    bok choy
4 tbsp lime juice
2 tbsp Thai fish sauce
1 tbsp soy sauce

TO GARNISH
2 tbsp fresh mint,
    shredded
slices of pickled garlic
fresh mint sprig

❶ Soak the rice noodles in hot water for 15 minutes, or according to the package directions. Drain well.

❷ Heat the oil in a wok or a large skillet and stir-fry the garlic, ginger, scallions, and chile for about 1 minute. Stir in the chicken and chicken livers, then stir-fry over a high heat for 2–3 minutes, or until beginning to brown.

❸ Stir in the celery and carrot, and stir-fry for 2 minutes to soften. Add the bok choy, then stir in the lime juice, fish sauce, and soy sauce.

❹ Add the noodles and stir to heat thoroughly. Sprinkle with shredded mint and pickled garlic. Serve immediately, garnished with a mint sprig.

 very easy

 serves 4

 15 minutes

 8 minutes

Chile Verde

2 lb 4 oz/1 kg pork, cut
    into bite-sized chunks
1 onion, chopped
2 bay leaves
1 whole garlic bulb,
    cut in half
1 bouillon cube
2 garlic cloves, chopped
1 lb/450 g fresh
    tomatillos, husks
    removed, cooked in a
    small amount of water
    until just tender, then
    chopped
2 large, mild green
    chiles, such as
    anaheim, or a
    combination of
    1 green bell pepper
    and 2 jalapeño chilis,
    deseeded and chopped
3 tbsp vegetable oil
1 cup pork or chicken
    bouillon
½ tsp mild chili powder—
    ancho or New Mexico
½ tsp cumin
4–6 tbsp chopped fresh
    cilantro, to garnish

TO SERVE
warmed flour tortillas
lime wedges

❶ Place the pork in a large pan with the onion, bay leaves, garlic bulb, and bouillon cube. Add water to cover and bring to a boil. Skim off the scum from the surface, then reduce the heat to very low and simmer gently for about 1½ hours, or until the meat is very tender.

❷ Meanwhile, put the chopped garlic in a blender or a food processor with the tomatillos and green chiles and pepper, if using. Process to a purée.

❸ Heat the oil in a pan, add the tomatillo mixture, and cook over a medium-high heat for about 10 minutes, or until thickened. Add the bouillon, chili powder, and cumin.

❹ When the meat is tender, remove from the pan and add to the sauce. Simmer gently to combine the flavors.

❺ Garnish with the chopped cilantro and serve with warmed tortillas and lime wedges.

 easy

 serves 4

 10 minutes

 2¼ hours

Steamed Chicken & Vegetable Packets

INGREDIENTS

4 boneless, skinless
chicken breasts
1 tsp ground lemon grass
2 scallions, chopped
finely
9 oz/250 g young carrots
9 oz/250 g young
zucchinis
2 celery stalks
1 tsp light soy sauce
9 oz/250 g spinach
leaves
2 tsp sesame oil
salt and pepper

❶ With a sharp knife, make a slit through one side of each chicken breast, to open out a large pocket. Sprinkle the inside of the pocket with lemon grass, salt, and pepper. Tuck the scallions into the pockets.

❷ Trim the carrots, zucchinis, and celery, then cut into short, thin sticks. Plunge into a pan of boiling water for 1 minute, then drain and toss in the soy sauce.

❸ Pack the vegetables into the pocket in each chicken breast and fold over firmly to enclose. Reserve any remaining vegetables. Wash the spinach leaves thoroughly, then drain and pat dry with paper towels. Wrap the chicken breasts firmly in the spinach leaves to enclose completely. If the leaves are too firm to wrap the chicken easily, steam them for a few seconds until they are softened and flexible.

❹ Place the wrapped chicken in a steamer and steam over rapidly boiling water for 20–25 minutes, depending on size.

❺ Stir-fry leftover vegetable sticks and spinach for 1–2 minutes in sesame oil, and serve with the chicken packets.

 easy

 serves 4

 25 minutes

 30 minutes

Italian Chicken Spirals

INGREDIENTS

4 skinless, boneless,
   chicken breasts
1 cup fresh basil leaves
2 tablespoons hazelnuts
1 garlic clove, crushed
2 cups whole-wheat
   pasta spirals
2 sun-dried tomatoes
   or fresh tomatoes
1 tbsp lemon juice
1 tbsp olive oil
1 tbsp capers
½ cup black olives
salt and pepper

❶ Beat the chicken breasts with a rolling pin to flatten them evenly.

❷ Place the basil and hazelnuts in a food processor and process until chopped finely. Mix with the garlic, salt, and pepper.

❸ Spread the basil mixture over the chicken breasts and roll up each breast from one short end to enclose the filling. Wrap each chicken roll tightly in foil so that all hold their shape, then seal the ends well.

❹ Bring a large pan of lightly salted water to a boil and cook the pasta until tender but still firm to the bite.

❺ Place the chicken parcels in a steamer basket or a colander set over the pan, then cover tightly and steam for 10 minutes. Meanwhile, dice the tomatoes.

❻ Drain the pasta and return it to the pan with the lemon juice, olive oil, tomatoes, capers, and olives. Heat through.

❼ Pierce the chicken with a skewer to make sure that the juices run clear and not pink, then slice the chicken and arrange over the pasta. Serve immediately.

easy

serves 4

10 minutes

15 minutes

Sauté of Chicken, Corn, & Snow Peas

4 skinless, boneless
  chicken breasts
9 oz/250 g baby corn
9 oz/250 g snow peas
2 tbsp sunflower oil
1 tbsp sherry vinegar
1 tbsp honey
1 tbsp light soy sauce
1 tbsp sunflower seeds
pepper
rice or egg noodles,
  to serve

❶ Using a sharp knife, slice the chicken breasts into long, thin strips. Cut the baby corn in half lengthwise, and trim the snow peas. Set the vegetables aside until required.

❷ Heat the sunflower oil in a wok or a wide skillet, and fry the chicken over a fairly high heat, stirring constantly, for 1 minute.

❸ Add the corn and snow peas and stir over a moderate heat for 5–8 minutes, or until evenly cooked.

❹ Mix together the sherry vinegar, honey, and soy sauce, and stir into the skillet with the sunflower seeds. Season with pepper to taste. Cook, stirring constantly, for 1 minute. Serve the sauté hot with rice or Chinese egg noodles.

extremely easy

serves 4

5–10 minutes

10 minutes

❶

❸

❹

COOK'S TIP
Rice vinegar or balsamic vinegar makes a good substitute for the sherry vinegar used in this sauté.

Skewered Spicy Tomato Chicken

❶ Using a sharp knife, cut the chicken into 1 inch/2.5 cm chunks and place in a bowl.

❷ Mix together the tomato paste, honey, Worcestershire sauce, and rosemary. Add to the chicken, stirring well to coat evenly.

❸ Alternating the chicken pieces and tomatoes, thread them onto eight wooden skewers. Spoon any remaining glaze over the skewers.

❹ Cook under a preheated hot broiler for 8–10 minutes, turning occasionally, until the chicken is thoroughly cooked. Serve on a bed of couscous or rice, and garnish with sprigs of rosemary.

 extremely easy

serves 4

5–10 minutes

8–10 minutes

❶  ❷  ❸

Warm Salad of Tuna & Tomatoes with Ginger Dressing

INGREDIENTS

½ cup bok choy, shredded
3 tbsp rice wine
2 tbsp Thai fish sauce
1 tbsp fresh ginger root, shredded finely
1 garlic clove, chopped finely
½ small red bird-eye chile, chopped finely
2 tsp soft light brown sugar
2 tbsp lime juice
14 oz/400 g fresh tuna steak
sunflower oil for brushing
1 cup cherry tomatoes
fresh mint leaves and mint sprigs, chopped coarsely, to garnish

❶ Place a small pile of shredded bok choy on a serving plate. Place the rice wine, fish sauce, ginger, garlic, chile, brown sugar, and 1 tablespoon lime juice in a screw-top jar and shake well to combine evenly.

❷ Cut the tuna into strips of an even thickness. Sprinkle with the remaining lime juice.

❸ Brush a wide skillet or griddle with the oil, and heat until very hot. Arrange the tuna strips in the skillet and cook until just firm and light golden, turning them over once. Remove and set aside.

❹ Add the tomatoes to the pan and cook over a high heat until lightly browned. Spoon the tuna and tomatoes over the bok choy, then spoon the dressing on top. Garnish with fresh mint and serve warm.

 extremely easy

 serves 4

 5 minutes

 5–10 minutes

Steamed Yellow Fish Fillets

1 lb 2 oz/500 g firm fish
    fillets, such as red
    snapper, sole, or
    monkfish
1 dried red bird-eye chili
1 small onion, chopped
3 garlic cloves, chopped
2 sprigs fresh cilantro
1 tsp coriander seeds
½ tsp turmeric
½ tsp ground black
    pepper
1 tbsp Thai fish sauce
2 tbsp coconut milk
1 small egg, beaten
2 tbsp rice flour
red and green chile
    strips, to garnish
soy sauce, to serve

 very easy

 serves 4

 10 minutes

12–15 minutes

❶ Remove any skin from the fish and cut the fillets diagonally into long ¾ inch/2 cm wide strips.

❷ Place the dried chili, onion, garlic, cilantro, and coriander seeds in a pestle and mortar, and grind them to a smooth paste.

❸ Add the turmeric, pepper, fish sauce, coconut milk, and beaten egg, stirring well to mix evenly.

❹ Dip the fish strips into the paste mixture, then into the rice flour to coat lightly.

❺ Bring the water in the bottom of a steamer to a boil, then arrange the fish strips in the top of the steamer. Cover and steam for about 12–15 minutes, or until the fish is just firm.

❻ Garnish the fish with the chile strips, then serve with soy sauce and stir-fried vegetables or salad.

COOK'S TIP
If you don't have a steamer, improvise by placing a large metal colander over a large pan of boiling water and cover with an upturned plate to enclose the fish as it steams.

Baked Cod with a Curry Crust

INGREDIENTS

½ tsp sesame oil
4 pieces cod fillet, about
    5½ oz/150 g each
1½ cups fresh white
    bread crumbs
2 tbsp blanched
    almonds, chopped
2 tsp Thai green curry
    paste
zest of ½ lime, finely
    grated
salt and pepper
boiled new potatoes,
    to serve
lime slices and zest, and
    mixed green leaves,
    to garnish

 extremely easy

 serves 4

 5 minutes

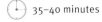 35–40 minutes

❶ Brush the sesame oil over the base of a wide, shallow ovenproof dish or pan, then place the pieces of cod in it, in a single layer.

❷ Mix the fresh bread crumbs, almonds, curry paste, and grated lime zest together, stirring well to blend thoroughly and evenly. Season to taste with salt and pepper.

❸ Carefully spoon the crumb mixture over the fish pieces, pressing lightly to hold it in place.

❹ Place the dish, uncovered, in a preheated oven at 400°F/200°C and bake for 35–40 minutes, or until the fish is cooked through and the crumb topping is golden brown.

❺ Serve the dish hot, garnished with lime slices and zest, and mixed green leaves, and accompanied by boiled new potatoes.

COOK'S TIP
To test whether the fish is cooked through, use a fork to pierce it in the thickest part—if the flesh is white all the way through and flakes apart easily, it is cooked sufficiently.

Salpicón of Crab

INGREDIENTS

¼ red onion, chopped
½–1 green chile,
    deseeded and
    chopped
juice of ½ lime
1 tbsp cider vinegar, or
    other fruit vinegar,
    such as raspberry
1 tbsp chopped fresh
    cilantro
1 tbsp extra-virgin olive
    oil
8–12 oz/225–350 g fresh
    crab meat
lettuce leaves, to serve

TO GARNISH
1 avocado
lime juice, for tossing
1–2 ripe tomatoes
3–5 radishes

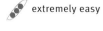 extremely easy

 serves 4

 10 minutes

0 minutes

❶ Combine the onion with the chile, lime juice, vinegar, fresh cilantro, and olive oil. Add the crab meat and toss the ingredients lightly together.

❷ To make the garnish, cut each avocado in half around the pit. Twist apart, then remove the pit with a knife. Carefully peel off the skin and slice the flesh. Toss the avocado gently in lime juice to prevent discoloration.

❸ Halve the tomatoes, then remove the cores and seeds. Dice the flesh. Slice the radishes thinly.

❹ Arrange the crab salad on a bed of lettuce leaves, then garnish with the avocado, tomatoes, and radishes. Serve at once.

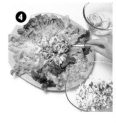

COOK'S TIP
For a toasted crab salad sandwich, split open a long roll or baguette and heap on crab salad. Top with a generous layer of cheese. Place the open roll under the broiler to melt the cheese. Spread the toasted plain side with a little mayonnaise and close the sandwich up. Serve with salsa.

Fish Burritos

 very easy

serves 4

5 minutes

45 minutes

❶ Season the fish with salt and pepper, then put in a pan with the cumin, oregano, garlic, and enough fish bouillon to cover all the ingredients.

❷ Bring to a boil, then cook for about a minute. Remove the pan from the heat and let the fish cool in the cooking liquid for about 30 minutes.

❸ Remove the fish from the bouillon and break it up into bite-sized pieces. Sprinkle the pieces with the lemon or lime juice, and set the fish aside.

❹ Heat the tortillas in an ungreased non-stick skillet, sprinkling them with a few drops of water as they heat. Remove them one by one from the pan as they heat and wrap them in a clean dish towel to keep them warm.

❺ Arrange shredded lettuce in the middle of one tortilla, spoon on a few big chunks of fish, then sprinkle with the tomato over the fish. Add Salsa Cruda. Repeat with the other tortillas and serve at once with lemon slices.

Cod Curry

INGREDIENTS

1 tbsp vegetable oil
1 small onion, chopped
2 garlic cloves, chopped
1 inch/2.5 cm piece fresh
   ginger, chopped coarsely
2 large ripe tomatoes,
   skinned and chopped
   coarsely
⅔ cup fish bouillon
1 tbsp medium curry paste
1 tsp ground coriander
14 oz/400 g canned
   garbanzo beans,
   drained and rinsed
1 lb 8 oz/675 g cod fillet,
   cut into large chunks
4 tbsp chopped cilantro
4 tbsp plain yogurt
salt and pepper
steamed basmati rice,
   to serve

❶ Heat the oil in a large pan and add the onion, garlic, and ginger. Fry for 4–5 minutes, or until softened. Remove from the heat. Put the onion mixture into a food processor or a blender with the tomatoes and fish bouillon, and blend until smooth.

❷ Return to the pan with the curry paste, ground coriander, and garbanzo beans. Mix together well, then simmer gently for 15 minutes, or until thickened.

❸ Add the pieces of fish and return to a simmer. Cook for 5 minutes, or until the fish is just tender. Remove from the heat and let stand for 2–3 minutes.

❹ Stir in the cilantro and yogurt. Season, and serve with steamed basmati rice.

 easy

 serves 4

 10 minutes

30 minutes

Barbecued Monkfish

INGREDIENTS

4 tbsp olive oil
grated zest of 1 lime
2 tsp Thai fish sauce
2 garlic cloves, crushed
1 tsp grated fresh ginger
*   root*
2 tbsp chopped fresh
*   basil*
1 lb 9 oz/700 g monkfish
*   fillet, cut into chunks*
2 limes, each cut into
*   6 wedges*
salt and pepper

❶ Mix together the olive oil, lime zest, fish sauce, garlic, ginger, and basil. Season and set aside.

❷ Wash and dry the fish. Add to the marinade and mix well. Let marinate for 2 hours, stirring occasionally.

❸ If you are using bamboo skewers, soak them in cold water for 30 minutes. Then lift the monkfish pieces from the marinade and thread them onto the skewers, alternating with the lime wedges.

❹ Transfer the skewers to a lit barbecue or to a preheated ridged grill pan. Cook for 5–6 minutes, turning regularly, until the fish is tender. Serve immediately.

 extremely easy

 serves 4

10 minutes,
plus 2 hours to
marinate

5–6 minutes

Stuffed Mackerel

INGREDIENTS

4 large mackerel,
    cleaned
1 tbsp olive oil
1 small onion, finely
    sliced
1 tsp ground cinnamon
½ tsp ground ginger
2 tbsp raisins
2 tbsp pine nuts, toasted
8 vine leaves in brine,
    drained
salt and pepper

❶ Wash and dry the fish and set aside. Heat the oil in a small skillet and add the onion. Cook gently for 5 minutes, or until softened. Add the cinnamon and ginger, and cook for 30 seconds before adding the raisins and pine nuts. Remove from the heat and let cool.

❷ Stuff each of the fish with a quarter of the stuffing mixture. Wrap each fish in 2 vine leaves, securing with toothpicks.

❸ Cook on a preheated barbecue or ridged grill pan for 5 minutes on each side, or until the vine leaves have scorched and the fish is tender. Serve immediately.

 very easy

 serves 4

 10 minutes

 12 minutes

Prawn & Asparagus Risotto

INGREDIENTS

5 cups vegetable
   bouillon
12 oz/350 g asparagus,
   cut into 2 inch/5 cm
   lengths
2 tbsp olive oil
1 onion, chopped finely
garlic clove, chopped
   finely
1½ cups arborio rice
1 lb/450g raw jumbo
   shrimp, peeled and
   deveined
2 tbsp olive paste or
   tapenade
2 tbsp chopped fresh basil
salt and pepper
Parmesan cheese, to
   garnish

❶ Bring the vegetable bouillon to a boil in a large pan. Add the asparagus and cook for 3 minutes, or until just tender. Strain, reserving the bouillon, and refresh the asparagus under cold running water. Drain and set aside.

❷ Heat the oil in a large skillet, add the onion, and cook gently for 5 minutes, or until softened. Add the garlic and cook for an additional 30 seconds. Add the rice and stir for 1–2 minutes, or until coated with the oil and slightly translucent.

❸ Keep the bouillon on a low heat. Increase the heat under the skillet to medium, and begin adding the bouillon a ladleful at a time, stirring well between additions. Continue until almost all the bouillon has been absorbed. This should take 20–25 minutes.

❹ Add the shrimp and asparagus with the last ladleful of bouillon and cook for an additional 5 minutes, or until the shrimp and rice are tender and the bouillon has been absorbed. Remove from the heat.

❺ Stir in the olive paste, basil, season, and let stand for 1 minute. Garnish with Parmesan shavings, and serve.

 easy

 serves 4

 10 minutes

 45 minutes

John Dory en Papillote

INGREDIENTS

2 John Dory, filleted
1 cup pitted black olives
12 cherry tomatoes,
*   halved*
4 oz/115 g green beans,
*   trimmed*
handful fresh basil
*   leaves*
4 slices fresh lemon
4 tsp olive oil
salt and pepper
fresh basil leaves,
*   to garnish*
boiled new potatoes,
*   to serve*

❶ Wash and dry the fish fillets and set aside. Cut 4 large rectangles of baking parchment measuring about 18 × 12 inches/ 45 × 30 cm. Fold in half to make a 9 × 12 inch/ 22.5 × 30 cm rectangle. Cut this into a large heart shape, and open it out.

❷ Lay one John Dory fillet on one half of the paper heart. Top with one-fourth of the olives, tomatoes, green beans, and basil, and one lemon slice. Drizzle 1 teaspoon of olive oil over the top and season well with salt and pepper.

❸ Fold over the other half of the paper and fold the edges of the paper together to enclose. Repeat to make 4 packets

❹ Place the packets on a cookie sheet and cook in a preheated oven at 400° F/200° C for 15 minutes, or until the fish is tender.

❺ Transfer each parcel unopened to a serving plate, and let your guests open their packets to enjoy the wonderful aroma. Suggest that they garnish their portions with fresh basil, and serve a generous helping of boiled new potatoes.

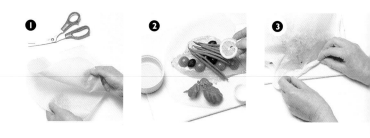

very easy

serves 4

15 minutes

15 minutes

Salads & Side Dishes

People are generally aware that most salads are composed of lowfat ingredients, but it may be a surprise to find such delicious combinations as in this section. Tuna Bean Salad is a fresh tuna steak on a bed of beans in a lemony olive-oil dressing— a medley of flavors. For an unusual side dish, try Fideos Tostados, rice and very thin pasta cooked together in a tomato sauce. Jasmine Rice with Lemon and Basil has a refreshing fragrance.

Jasmine Rice with Lemon & Basil

INGREDIENTS

1 cup jasmine rice
1¾ cups water
zest of ¼ lemon, grated
    finely
2 tbsp fresh sweet basil,
    chopped

❶ Wash the rice in several changes of cold water until the water runs clear. Bring the water to a boil in a large pan, then add the rice.

❷ Bring back to a rolling boil. Turn the heat to a low simmer, then cover the pan and simmer for another 12 minutes.

❸ Remove the pan from the heat and let stand, covered, for 10 minutes.

❹ Fluff up the rice with a fork, then stir in the lemon. Serve scattered with basil.

 extremely easy

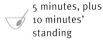 serves 4

 5 minutes, plus 10 minutes' standing

20 minutes

COOK'S TIP

It is important to leave the pan tightly covered while the rice cooks and steams inside, so that the grains cook evenly and become fluffy and separate.

Thai-Style Carrot & Mango Salad

INGREDIENTS

4 carrots
1 small, ripe mango
200 g/7 oz firm bean
   curd
1 tbsp fresh chives,
   chopped

DRESSING

2 tbsp orange juice
1 tbsp lime juice
1 tsp clear honey
½ tsp orange-flower
   water
1 tsp sesame oil
1 tsp sesame seeds,
   toasted

❶ Peel the carrots and grate them coarsely. Peel the mango, pit it and slice it thinly.

❷ Cut the tofu into ½ inch/1 cm cubes and toss it with the carrots and mango in a wide salad bowl.

❸ For the dressing, place all the ingredients in a screw-top jar and shake well to mix evenly.

❹ Pour the dressing over the salad and toss well to coat the salad evenly.

❺ Just before serving, toss the salad lightly and sprinkle it with chives. Serve immediately.

 extremely easy

serves 4

10 minutes

0 minutes

COOK'S TIP
A food processor will grate the carrots in seconds, so it is a useful time-saving device if you are catering for a large number of people.

Tuna Bean Salad

INGREDIENTS

1 cup dried navy beans
1 tbsp lemon juice
5 tbsp extra-virgin olive
 oil, plus extra for
 brushing
1 garlic clove, chopped
 finely
1 small red onion, sliced
 very finely (optional)
1 tbsp chopped fresh
 parsley
6 oz/175 g tuna steaks
salt and pepper

TO GARNISH
parsley sprigs
lemon wedges

 very easy

 serves 4

10 minutes,
plus 8 hours
to soak beans

2 hours

❶ Soak the navy beans for 8 hours or overnight in at least twice their volume of cold water.

❷ When you are ready to cook, drain the beans and place them in a pan with twice their volume of fresh water. Bring slowly to a boil, skimming off any scum that rises to the surface. Boil the beans rapidly for 10 minutes, then reduce the heat and simmer for an additional 1¼–1½ hours, or until the beans are tender.

❸ Meanwhile, mix together the lemon juice, olive oil, garlic, and seasoning. Drain the beans thoroughly, and toss them in the olive oil mixture, the onion, and the parsley. Season to taste and set aside.

❹ Wash and dry the tuna steaks. Brush lightly with olive oil, and season. Cook on a preheated ridged grill pan for 2 minutes on each side until they are just pink in the center.

❺ Divide the bean salad between 4 serving plates. Top each with a tuna steak. Garnish with parsley sprigs and lemon wedges, and serve immediately.

COOK'S TIP
You could use canned navy beans instead of dried. Reheat according to the instructions on the can, then drain and toss with the dressing as above.

Spiced Lentils with Spinach

INGREDIENTS

2 tbsp olive oil
1 large onion, chopped finely
1 large garlic clove, crushed
½ tbsp ground cumin
½ tsp ground ginger
1¼ cups Puy lentils
about 2½ cups vegetable
  or chicken bouillon
3½ oz/100 g baby
  spinach leaves
2 tbsp fresh mint leaves
1 tbsp fresh cilantro leaves
1 tbsp fresh flatleaf
  parsley leaves
freshly squeezed
  lemon juice
salt and pepper
grated lemon zest,
  to garnish

 easy

 serves 4

10 minutes

35 minutes

❶ Heat the olive oil in a large skillet over a medium–high heat. Add the onion and cook for about 6 minutes. Stir in the garlic, cumin, and ginger, and continue cooking, stirring occasionally, until the onion just starts to brown.

❷ Stir in the lentils. Pour in enough bouillon to cover the lentils by 1 inch/2.5 cm and bring to a boil. Lower the heat and simmer for 20 minutes, or according to the instructions on the packet, until the lentils are tender.

❸ Meanwhile, rinse the spinach leaves in several changes of cold water and shake dry. Chop the mint, cilantro, and parsley leaves finely.

❹ If there is no bouillon left in the pan, add a little extra. Add the spinach and stir through until it just wilts. Stir in the mint, cilantro, and parsley. Adjust the seasoning, adding lemon juice and salt and pepper. Transfer to a serving bowl and serve, garnished with lemon zest.

COOK'S TIP
This recipe uses green lentils from Puy in France because they are good at keeping their shape even after long cooking. You can, however, also use orange or brown lentils, but it is necessary to watch them while they cook or they will quickly turn to a mush.

Zucchinis & Tomatoes with Green Chile Vinaigrette

INGREDIENTS

1 large fresh mild green chile, or a combination of 1 green bell pepper and ½–1 fresh green chile
4 zucchinis, sliced
2–3 garlic cloves, chopped finely
pinch sugar
¼ tsp ground cumin
2 tbsp white wine vinegar
4 tbsp extra-virgin olive oil
2–3 tbsp cilantro
4 ripe tomatoes, diced or sliced
salt and pepper

❶ Roast the mild chile, or the combination of the green bell pepper and chile, in a heavy-based ungreased skillet or under a preheated grill until the skin is charred. Place in a plastic bag, twist to seal well, then let the mixture stand for 20 minutes.

❷ Peel the skin from the chile and pepper, if using, then remove the seeds and slice the flesh. Set aside.

❸ Bring about 2 inches/5 cm water to a boil in the bottom of a steamer. Add the zucchinis to the top part of the steamer, then cover and steam for about 5 minutes, or until just tender.

❹ Meanwhile, thoroughly combine the garlic, sugar, cumin, vinegar, olive oil, and cilantro in a bowl. Stir in the chile and pepper, if using, then season with salt and pepper to taste.

❺ Arrange the zucchinis and tomatoes in a serving bowl or on a plate, and spoon the chile dressing over them. Toss gently, and serve.

 easy

 serves 4

 10 minutes, plus 20 minutes to stand

 10 minutes

Potatoes in Green Sauce

INGREDIENTS

2 lb 4 oz/1 kg small waxy
  potatoes, peeled
1 onion, halved and
  unpeeled
8 garlic cloves, unpeeled
1 green chile
8 tomatillos, outer husks
  removed, or small tart
  tomatoes
1 cup chicken, meat, or
  vegetable bouillon,
  preferably home made
½ tsp ground cumin
1 sprig fresh thyme or
  generous pinch dried
1 sprig fresh oregano or
  generous pinch dried
2 tbsp vegetable or
  extra-virgin olive oil
1 bunch fresh cilantro,
  chopped
1 zucchini, chopped
  coarsely
salt

❶ Put the potatoes in a pan of salted water. Bring to a boil and cook for about 15 minutes, or until almost tender. Do not over-cook them. Drain and set aside.

❷ Lightly char the onion, garlic, chili, and tomatillos or tomatoes in a heavy-based ungreased skillet. Set aside, and when cool enough to handle, peel and chop the onion, garlic, and chile. Chop the tomatillos or tomatoes. Place all the ingredients in a blender or a food processor with half the bouillon, and process to form a purée. Add the cumin, thyme, and oregano.

❸ Heat the oil in the heavy-based skillet. Add the purée and cook for 5 minutes, stirring, to reduce slightly and concentrate the flavors.

❹ Add the potatoes, and chopped zucchini to the purée, and pour in the rest of the bouillon. Add about half the cilantro and cook for another 5 minutes, or until the zucchini pieces are tender.

❺ Transfer to a serving bowl and serve sprinkled with the remaining chopped cilantro to garnish.

easy

serves 4

20 minutes

30 minutes

Fresh Pineapple Salsa

INGREDIENTS

1 small ripe pineapple
juice of 1 lime or lemon
1 garlic clove, chopped
   finely
1 scallion,
   thinly sliced
½–1 green or red chile,
   deseeded and
   chopped finely
½ red pepper, deseeded
   and chopped
3 tbsp chopped fresh
   mint
3 tbsp chopped fresh
   cilantro
pinch of salt
pinch of sugar

❶ Using a sharp knife, cut off the top and bottom of the pineapple. Place upright on a board, then slice off the skin, cutting downward. Cut the flesh into slices, halve the slices, and remove the cores, if wished. Dice the flesh. Reserve any juice that accumulates as you cut the pineapple.

❷ Place the pineapple in a bowl and stir in the lime juice, garlic, scallion, chopped chile, and red bell pepper.

❸ Stir in the chopped fresh mint and cilantro. Add the salt and sugar, and stir well to combine all the ingredients. Chill until ready to serve.

 extremely easy

 serves 4

 15 minutes

 0 minutes

Fideos Tostados

INGREDIENTS

12 oz/350 g vermicelli or
   angel hair pasta in
   coils, coarsely broken
½ cup long-grain white
   rice
3 tbsp extra-virgin olive
   oil
7 oz/200 g canned
   chopped tomatoes,
   drained
2½ cups chicken bouillon
   or water, plus extra if
   necessary
1 bay leaf
1–2 tsp chopped fresh
   oregano or 1 tsp dried
   oregano
½ tsp dried thyme leaves
salt and pepper
1–2 tbsp sprigs and
   chopped fresh
   oregano or thyme,
   to garnish

❶ Put the pasta and rice in a dry, large, heavy-based pan or flameproof casserole over a medium-high heat and cook for 5–7 minutes, stirring frequently, until light golden. (The pasta will break unevenly, but this does not matter.)

❷ Stir in 2 tablespoons of the olive oil, together with the chopped tomatoes, bouillon, bay leaf, oregano, and thyme, then season with about a teaspoon of salt and pepper to taste.

❸ Bring to a boil, then reduce the heat to medium and simmer for about 8 minutes, stirring frequently, to help unwind and separate the pasta coils.

❹ Reduce the heat to low and then cook, covered, for about 10 minutes, or until the rice and pasta are tender and all the liquid is absorbed. If the rice and pasta are too firm, add about ½ cup more bouillon or water, and continue to cook, covered, for another 5 minutes. Remove from the heat.

❺ Using a fork, fluff the rice and pasta into a warmed deep serving bowl and drizzle with the remaining oil. Sprinkle with the herbs and serve immediately.

 very easy

 serves 4

5 minutes

30–35 minutes

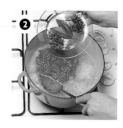

Desserts

With a little thought (and discipline) it is possible to create a low-fat dessert that looks and tastes wonderful. Espresso Granita is ice flavored with coffee or vanilla, served in chilled bowls. It is fat-free, yet it makes a perfect end to a special meal. In the following pages you can also find Chocolate & Raspberry Vacherin, an impressive dessert for an occasion, a low-fat meringue layered with melted chocolate and crème frâiche, and a reduced-fat Chocolate Mousse. Fruit is an equally delicious but less indulgent alternative. In this section you will find it combined imaginatively with potato in Fruity Potato Cake, and with pasta in Raspberry Fusilli.

Lychee & Ginger Sorbet

INGREDIENTS

1 lb 12 oz/800 g canned
    lychees in syrup
zest of 1 lime, grated
    finely
2 tbsp lime juice
3 tbsp preserved ginger
    syrup
2 egg whites

TO DECORATE
starfruit slices
slivers of stem ginger

❶ Drain the lychees, reserving the syrup. Place the fruits in a blender or a food processor with the lime zest, juice, and the preserved ginger syrup, then process until completely smooth. Transfer to a mixing bowl.

❷ Mix the purée thoroughly with the reserved syrup, then pour into a freezerproof container and freeze for 1–1½ hours, or until slushy in texture. (Alternatively, use an ice-cream maker.)

❸ Remove from the freezer and whisk to break up the ice crystals. Whisk the egg whites in a clean, dry bowl until stiff, then quickly and lightly fold into the iced mixture.

❹ Return to the freezer and freeze until firm. Serve the sorbet in scoops, with slices of starfruit and ginger to decorate.

 very easy

 serves 4

 10 minutes, plus
    1–1½ hours
    to freeze

 0 minutes

COOK'S TIP

It is not recommended that raw egg whites are served to very young children, pregnant women, the elderly, or anyone weakened by chronic illness. The egg whites may be left out, but you should whisk the sorbet a second time after another hour of freezing.

Fruity potato cake

INGREDIENTS

1 lb 8 oz/675 g sweet
   potatoes, diced
1 tbsp butter, melted
²/₃ cup brown
   crystal sugar
3 eggs
3 tbsp milk
1 tbsp lemon juice
grated rind of 1 lemon
1 tsp caraway seeds
²/₃ cup dried fruits, such
   as apple, pear or
   mango, chopped
2 tsp baking powder

❶ Grease a 7 inch/18 cm square cake pan lightly.

❷ Cook the sweet potatoes in boiling water for 10 minutes or until soft. Drain and mash the sweet potatoes until they form a smooth mixture.

❸ Transfer the mashed sweet potatoes to a mixing bowl while they are still hot and add the butter and sugar, mixing well to dissolve the sugar.

❹ Beat in the eggs, lemon juice and rind, caraway seeds, and chopped dried fruit. Add the baking powder and mix well.

❺ Pour the mixture into the prepared cake pan.

❻ Cook the cake in a preheated oven, 325°F/160°C, for 1–1¼ hours, or until it is cooked through. Remove the cake from the pan and transfer it to a wire rack to cool. Cut it into thick slices to serve.

easy

makes one 7 inch/ 18 cm cake

20 minutes

1–1¼ hours

COOK'S TIP

This cake is ideal as a dessert for a special occasion. It can be made in advance, then wrapped in plastic wrap and frozen until required. Thaw at room temperature for 24 hours and then warm through in a moderate oven before serving.

Raspberry Fusilli

INGREDIENTS

6 oz/175 g fusilli pasta
4 cups raspberries
2 tbsp superfine sugar
1 tbsp lemon juice
4 tbsp slivered almonds
3 tbsp raspberry liqueur

❶ Bring a large pan of lightly salted water to a boil. Add the fusilli and cook until tender but still firm to the bite. Drain the fusilli thoroughly, return to the pan and set aside to cool.

❷ Using a spoon, firmly press 1⅓ cups of the raspberries through a strainer set over a large mixing bowl to form a smooth purée.

❸ Put the raspberry purée and sugar in a small pan and simmer over a low heat, stirring occasionally, for 5 minutes. Stir in the lemon juice and set the sauce aside until required.

❹ Add the remaining raspberries to the fusilli in the pan and mix well. Transfer the raspberry and fusilli mixture to a serving dish.

❺ Spread the almonds out on a cookie sheet and toast under the broiler until golden brown. Remove and set aside to cool slightly.

❻ Stir the raspberry liqueur into the reserved raspberry sauce and mix together well until very smooth. Pour the raspberry sauce over the fusilli, then generously sprinkle over the toasted almonds and serve.

 easy

 serves 4

 10 minutes

20 minutes

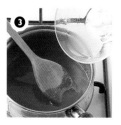

Chocolate & Raspberry Vacherin

INGREDIENTS

3 egg whites
¾ cup superfine sugar
1 tsp cornstarch
1 oz/25 g semisweet
  chocolate, grated

FILLING
6 oz/175 g semisweet
  chocolate
2 cups half-fat crème
  fraîche
2 cups fresh raspberries
a little melted chocolate,
  to decorate

❶ Draw 3 rectangles, 10 × 25 cm/4 × 10 inches, on sheets of baking parchment and place on 2 cookie sheets.

❷ Whisk the egg whites in a bowl until they stand in peaks. Whisk in half the sugar gradually, and whisk until stiff and glossy. Fold in the rest of the sugar, the cornstarch, and the grated chocolate with a metal spoon or spatula.

❸ Spoon the mixture into a piping bag fitted with a ½ inch/1 cm plain nozzle and pipe lines across the rectangles.

❹ Bake in a preheated oven, 275°F/140°C, for 1½ hours. Change the positions of the cookie sheets halfway through. When cooked, turn off the oven, leaving the door closed, to let the meringues cool inside, then peel off the parchment.

❺ To make the filling, melt the chocolate and spread it over 2 of the meringue layers. Let the filling harden.

❻ Place 1 chocolate-coated meringue on a plate and top with about one-third of the crème fraîche and raspberries. Gently place the second chocolate-coated meringue on top and spread with half the remaining crème fraîche and fruit.

❼ Place and decorate the last meringue layer as in step 6, then drizzle melted chocolate over the top, and serve.

easy

serves 4

25 minutes

1½ hours

❶

❸

❻

Chocolate Mousse

INGREDIENTS

3½ oz/100 g semisweet chocolate, melted
⅔ cup plain yogurt
⅔ cup Quark lowfat curd cheese
4 tbsp superfine sugar
1 tbsp orange juice
1 tbsp brandy
1½ tsp gelatine
9 tbsp cold water
2 large egg whites
coarsely grated dark and white chocolate and orange zest, to decorate

very easy

serves 4

10 minutes, plus 2 hours to chill

5 minutes

COOKS TIP
For a quick fruit sauce, blend a can of mandarin segments in natural juice in a food processor and press through a strainer. Stir in 1 tbsp clear honey and serve with the mousse.

❶ Put the melted chocolate, plain yogurt, Quark lowfat curd cheese, superfine sugar, orange juice, and brandy in a food processor, and blend for 30 seconds. Transfer the mixture to a large bowl.

❷ Sprinkle the gelatine over the water and stir until dissolved.

❸ In a small pan, bring the gelatine and water to a boil for 2 minutes. Let cool slightly, then stir into the chocolate mixture.

❹ Whisk the egg whites until stiff peaks form, and fold into the chocolate mixture using a metal spoon.

❺ Line a 1½ pint/850 ml loaf tin with plastic wrap. Spoon the mousse into the tin. Chill for 2 hours in the refrigerator until set. Turn the mousse out onto a plate, decorate with white chocolate and orange zest, and serve.

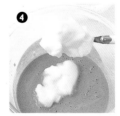

Espresso Granita

INGREDIENTS

1 cup superfine sugar
2½ cups water
½ tsp vanilla essence
2½ cups very strong
   espresso coffee,
   chilled
fresh mint, to garnish

❶ Put the sugar in a pan with the water and stir over a low heat to dissolve the sugar. Increase the heat and boil for 4 minutes, without stirring. Use a wet pastry brush to brush down any spatters on the side of the pan.

❷ Remove the pan from the heat and pour the syrup into a heatproof non-metal bowl. Sit the bowl in the kitchen sink filled with iced water to speed up the cooling process. Stir in the vanilla and coffee, and let stand until completely cool.

❸ Transfer to a shallow metal container, then cover and freeze. (It will keep for up to 3 months.)

❹ Thirty minutes before serving, place serving bowls in the refrigerator to chill.

❺ To serve, invert the container onto a cutting board. Rinse a cloth in very hot water and wring it out, then rub it on the bottom of the container for 15 seconds. Give the container a sharp shake and the mixture should fall out. If not, repeat.

❻ Use a knife to break up the granita and transfer it to a food processor. Quickly process until it becomes grainy and crunchy. Serve at once in the chilled bowls, decorated with mint.

 very easy

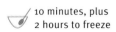 serves 4

 10 minutes, plus
2 hours to freeze

10 minutes